YOUNG READERS

LORD, I WANT TO KNOW YOU BETTER

Story Devotions for Boys

Stephen W. Sorenson

AUGSBURG Publishing House • Minneapolis

LORD, I WANT TO KNOW YOU BETTER

Copyright © 1982 Augsburg Publishing House

Library of Congress Catalog Card No. 81-052280

International Standard Book No. 0-8066-1912-0

Scripture quotations marked NIV are from the Holy Bible: New International Version. Copyright 1978 by the New York International Bible Society. Used by permission of Zondervan Bible Publishers.

LB refers to The Living Bible © 1971 by Tyndale House Publishers.

Illustrations: Koechel/Peterson Design

MANUFACTURED IN THE UNITED STATES OF AMERICA

To Aunt Helen Borgmeier,
whose love and encouragement
has meant a lot to me
and to many others.

Contents

About This Book

When you meet a new friend who is fun to be with, it's important that you spend time with each other. The more you do together—bike riding, playing games, reading, exploring—the better you will get to know each other and the deeper your relationship will become.

Getting to know the Lord better is important too. He wants to be your best friend, and he'll be with you always, no matter where you are. After you become a Christian and your relationship with God begins, there's much more for you to learn about him. Just as you talk to your friends and your family, you need to talk to God in prayer and read the Bible. God will reveal himself to you every day. He will guide you in making decisions and love you when it seems no one else really cares. When you pray, he will answer you. When you reach out to someone who is lonely, he will be there to encourage you. When you have a hard time getting along with your parents or your brothers or sisters, he will help you.

In the following pages, you will read stories about boys your age who are growing up and learning what it means to know God better. They learn how to get along with other people, laugh, learn new ideas, and make mistakes. And they learn more about themselves and others around them.

I wrote this book in the hope that it will help you learn, as I have, how wonderful God is. Have fun reading the stories, and pass this book along to your friends after you're done reading it! But most important, get to know God better. Take time to be with him, to learn more about him through Bible reading and prayer. When you do, you'll start an adventure that'll be even more exciting than the stories in this book.

Trapped!

"I'm tired of looking in these stores, Don," Jim complained to his brother. "I thought Cripple Creek would have a lot more neat things to see, instead of high-priced souvenirs for tourists."

"Yeah. Let's go explore in the hills," Don said. He hopped on his bicycle. "We're only going to be here until tomorrow, when Dad finishes his meetings in Denver."

"Where do you want to go?" Dennis Riley asked his cousins. "I told my parents we'd be back by 5:00."

"Let's go down this road." Jim pedaled hard and then coasted down the hill, with the other two boys trailing behind. After several blocks, he turned right onto a dirt road.

"There sure are lots of rocks," Don said. "I hope I don't bend the rim on my front wheel." The boys rode past a huge mound of purple, yellow, and green-shaded rocks.

"How did the miners get these rocks out of the mine shafts?" Jim asked.

"Back in the early 1890s they used picks and shovels," Dennis replied. "Sometimes they built wooden braces called 'cribbing' to hold up the tunnels. Before electricity was brought in, the miners had to crank the ore buckets out by hand. By 1894, there were more than 100 mines in this area."

"What's that thing?" Jim pointed.

"It's an ore chute. The miners sent ore down the chutes into wagons. After the railroads began stopping here regularly, the miners shoveled the ore from the wagons into railroad cars to be shipped to the mills."

Jim laid his bicycle down and began climbing up a steep rocky slope. "I'm going to explore." He climbed halfway up. "Aren't you guys coming?"

"OK." Dennis and Don began climbing too.

"I'm sure glad I didn't have to shovel all this rock," Don said.

"So am I." Dennis looked back at the hills of tailings. "My father told me that a person loading ore into a wagon was expected to move more than 35 tons of rock a day!"

When Dennis reached the top, he waited for Don, and the two of them walked toward the old buildings.

"Hey, Jim, where are you?" Don called out.

"In here."

Dennis walked toward the largest building. The tin roof and walls had partially collapsed. "Where are you?" Don asked again.

"Right here." Jim popped his head up from underneath some boards in a fenced-in area. "I'm exploring this old mine shaft."

"Get out of there!" Dennis exclaimed. "Right now. It's dangerous."

"What's wrong?" Jim asked. "Are you afraid to climb down here with me?"

"That fence is there to keep people out. How'd you get over it?"

"I climbed. What do you think?" Jim grinned. "It's really neat down here. There are lots of old boards, and in the center there's a big hole."

"Jim, will you please climb out of there?" Dennis walked closer, trying to stay calm. "That mine shaft isn't safe. A lot of those boards are probably rotten, and the sides could cave in."

"You're just afraid to admit that you've never done this." Jim ducked back down. "I'm going to see what's under here no matter what you say."

"Jim," Dennis' voice was louder, "climb out of there. There are lots of other neat places to see that aren't dangerous."

"He's right," Don said, putting his hand on the fence. "Let's go farther up the road."

"I've been climbing around old houses for years," Jim bragged, and the two boys could hear him moving boards. "I bet I know more about places like this than you do."

"Maybe you do," Dennis said, "even though I've lived here all my life. You don't have to prove anything to us. Just climb out before you get hurt."

Jim's voice was muffled. "I won't get hurt, but I'm sure glad I brought a flashlight."

Suddenly several boards on top fell in, and piles of dirt slid down. Jim cried out and then was silent.

"Are you OK?" Dennis shouted. He listened carefully and thought he heard a moan. He grabbed

Don's arm. "You can't help him by getting trapped in there too. Stay right here in case he starts talking. If he does, tell him not to move at all. Do you understand?" Dennis looked Don in the eye. "And don't try to do anything yourself."

"I understand." Don's voice wavered. "Will he be all right?"

"I don't know. I'm going to get help." Dennis ran to his bicycle and pedaled furiously to the sheriff's office. "Sheriff Douglas," he blurted out, breathing heavily, "my cousin is trapped in a mine shaft. He climbed in and something happened."

"Which one?"

"The first one off the old Shelf Road."

The sheriff telephoned several people and then grabbed a flashlight and a coil of rope.

"My other cousin is there to show you where Jim is," Dennis said. "I've got to tell my parents. I warned Jim, but he wouldn't listen."

"Let me handle things now," the sheriff said, hurrying out the door. "You've done the best you could."

Dennis jumped back on his bicycle. A few minutes later, he and his parents were driving to the mine shaft. "Didn't you tell him not to go in there?" his mother asked.

"I did, I did." Tears smudged Dennis' cheeks. "He climbed up there first and went in before I could stop him. And when I told him to get out, he laughed at me. He wouldn't listen."

"I hope he's not too far down," his father said.

"I think I heard him moan after it caved in," Dennis replied. "He must be near the top."

"Thank God for that." The three of them jumped

out of the car and ran up the slope. Don met them at the top.

"Two men are inside," Don said, "and those guys on top are helping too. Jim started talking just after you left, and I told him not to move. The dirt was sliding into the hole, and every time Jim moved the whole pile started moving again. I told him not to talk and to be as still as he could." Don clenched his fists. "I wanted to get down and help him but . . . . "

"You did the right thing," Mr. Riley reassured him.

"He wouldn't listen to me," Dennis repeated.

"It isn't your fault, Dennis." His mother gave him a hug. "You got help and did everything you could. Now it's up to the men. They're trained to do this." Her voice broke and she looked away.

The family stood close together, silently. The faraway sound of a siren grew louder and louder, and soon an ambulance pulled in behind the other cars. "How is it down there?" Mr. Riley asked.

"It's not good, but the boy is conscious," a volunteer fireman said. "His head is bleeding, and his leg is pinned under a beam. There's a lot of loose dirt over him."

A few minutes later, the fireman continued, "The sheriff has tied a rope around the boy's waist. In a minute we'll get the beam off his leg." A chain saw sputtered and then started. A thin cloud of blue smoke drifted out the top of the shaft.

"Lower the stretcher."

Two men swung the stretcher into the hole. After what seemed like hours, they lifted Jim out of the shaft's entrance. Then the ambulance attendants carefully carried him down to the ambulance.

"Should I ride along?" Mrs. Riley asked.

14

"Get in!" As soon as she climbed inside, the door slammed shut.

"He was lucky," the sheriff said, watching the ambulance drive off. "He nearly fell into the shaft."

"How deep is it?" Don asked. "A hundred feet?"

"More than 1000 feet."

Don looked back at the fence as a volunteer fireman finished putting a section back up. "Maybe the fence should be higher."

"It wouldn't make any difference." Sheriff Douglas sighed. "There's always somebody who won't pay attention to signs and will climb into a place like this. Thank God Jim is safe."

No one else said anything as they walked to their cars.

> The way of a fool seems right to him, but a wise man listens to advice.
>
> Proverbs 12:15 NIV

Lord, sometimes I don't want to listen to advice. I want to do things my own way. I'm tempted to show off so I can prove that I'm not afraid, that I'm part of the group. Help me realize it's good to be afraid sometimes and that I don't have to act one way when I'm really very different on the inside. A real friend will accept me the way I am.

What If You Get Caught?

It was nearly noon when the two boys paused in front of Mason's Sport and Hobby Store. "Hey, Jeff, let's go in here. I want to buy a model airplane," Kevin said. The short, red-haired boy moved toward the door.

"OK," Jeff answered, "but we can't stay too long. My brother said he'd take us skating after lunch."

The boys walked down the long center aisle, glancing at the sale items. Then Kevin walked two aisles over and stopped in front of the model kits. "Look at this one," he said, picking up a box and looking at the airplane on the cover. "It's a Republic P-47D Thunderbolt, the kind they used to fly during World War II."

"Let me see it," Jeff said, walking up from behind. As Kevin handed him the model, Jeff slipped it under his jacket.

"Why did you do that?" Kevin whispered. "I have to take it up to the cash register."

"No you don't," Jeff stated, a grin spreading across his face. "You won't even have to pay for it."

Kevin stared at Jeff in disbelief. "You mean you're going to steal it?"

"Hey, don't talk so loud." Jeff looked up and down the aisle and then said, "Sure. Everybody does it."

Kevin's heart beat faster. "Well, I don't," he said. "Stealing isn't right. Put it back before someone sees you."

"Don't worry," Jeff said. "There's just that one lady, and she's a customer. Nobody will know. Besides, the store won't miss it anyway."

"I still don't think you should steal it," Kevin answered, hoping that nobody could overhear them. "What if you get caught?"

"I won't. I've done this lots of times with other kids, and nobody has gotten caught yet." Jeff headed confidently for the door, but Kevin trailed behind, not knowing what else to do.

Suddenly the woman who had been in the next aisle rushed past Kevin and blocked the front door. "That's far enough, boys," she said. "Please come with me."

For a moment Jeff looked as if he were going to try to run out the door anyway, but the woman's look stopped him. "Yeah, we'll come," he finally said, "but what for? We haven't done anything wrong."

The woman followed them closely as they walked back down the aisle. When they reached the end, she said, "Now go through this door."

Jeff pushed open the door, and a man behind a desk stood up. "I'm Harry Mason, the owner of this store," he said. "Sit down in those green chairs next to the wall." After the boys sat down, he continued, "Mrs. Olson is my security guard. Do you have something in your pockets that isn't yours? Please lay everything on the floor."

Kevin quickly pulled out several dollar bills and a small pocketknife, but Jeff hesitated. "Why do we have to do this?" he asked.

"Please unzip your jacket and show me what's in your pockets," Mr. Mason said firmly.

Jeff unzipped the jacket slowly, a frightened look in his eyes. "Now what?"

"Hold open the sides."

Jeff pulled the jacket open, and Mr. Mason saw the model airplane box tucked into the large inside pocket. "Take that out of your pocket and give it to me." Carrying the model, Mr. Mason walked to his desk. "Now I have to call the police and let them handle this."

"They won't call my parents, will they?" Kevin asked, gripping the sides of his chair.

"I don't know, son." Mr. Mason picked up the telephone receiver and dialed.

"I didn't mean to take the model," Jeff whined, "and I'll be glad to put it back!"

"You should have thought of that before you took it." Mr. Mason finished dialing the number and let it ring. "Officer Melvin, this is Harry Mason at the sport and hobby store. I'd like you to send someone over here to deal with two boys we just caught shoplifting." Turning to Mrs. Olson, he said, "It's OK. I'll watch them until the police get here."

Kevin and Jeff looked at one another. "I don't think

he can do much to us," Jeff whispered. "A lot of kids do this."

"But what if the police do come, and he isn't just trying to scare us?" Kevin asked. "What do we do then?"

"Please sit still and be quiet," Mr. Mason said.

Minutes later, a policeman pushed the door open. "I'm Officer Keyser," he said, looking at the boys. "What seems to be the problem?"

"My security guard caught them stealing a model airplane," Mr. Mason replied. "The blond-haired boy had it under his jacket and was carrying it out the door."

"What is your name?" Officer Keyser asked, looking at Jeff, "and where do you live?"

"Jeff Schrader. I live at 1015 Fontmore Road."

"Are your parents home now?"

"Just my mother."

As Officer Keyser picked up the telephone book, Jeff stood up. "You're not going to call my parents, are you? I didn't mean to take the model."

"I'm afraid that I have to inform your parents before we can go any further," Officer Keyser said, holding the receiver up to his ear. "Hello, Mrs. Schrader? This is Officer Keyser with the Upton Police Department. Your son is being detained for shoplifting at Mason's, and I'd like you to come here right away." After he hung up, the policeman turned to Kevin. "I need the same information from you. Even though it appears that you didn't actually take the model, I still have to call your parents."

"Do you have to?"

The officer nodded.

"I'm Kevin Walker, and I live at 4595 Meadow-lane."

After calling Kevin's home and talking with Mr. Walker, Officer Keyser turned to the boys again. "I'll wait until your parents get here before asking you any more questions," he said. "But I want you to know that you're in pretty big trouble."

Looking confused, Mrs. Schrader and Mr. Walker entered the back room about 15 minutes later. "Is it true?" Mrs. Schrader asked, looking hard at Jeff. "Did you really do that?"

"Before he answers," Officer Keyser interrupted, "I need to make sure that both you and your son know your legal rights. Jeff, you have the right to remain silent," he stated, "and if you give up your right to remain silent, anything you say can and will be used against you in a court of law. You have the right to have a lawyer present during any questioning, and if you can't afford a lawyer one will be appointed by the court prior to any questioning. Do you understand that?"

"Yes," Jeff said, looking up at his mother and then down at the tile floor. Officer Keyser then repeated the same statement for Kevin and his father, and Kevin said that he understood it too.

"Now," Officer Keyser continued, "did you steal the model, Jeff?"

"It was in my jacket pocket," Jeff said quietly, his face turning red.

"Did you steal it?" Officer Keyser repeated.

"I didn't take it outside the store, if that's what you mean," Jeff said. "I wasn't even out the front door. You can't accuse me of stealing it."

"But you were going to steal it, weren't you?"

"Yes," Jeff replied, "but it's only a two-dollar model airplane. What's the big deal?"

"Well," Officer Keyser said, "you and your friend are guilty of theft even though you didn't carry the model outside. You intended to steal it, and that's what matters."

"But I didn't do anything," Kevin said, looking down at his gym shoes to avoid looking at his father. "I didn't steal anything."

"But weren't you with Jeff?" Officer Keyser asked. When Kevin nodded, he went on, "You didn't stop him from stealing the model even though you could have."

"I did tell him to put it back before someone saw him," Kevin said defensively.

"But," Officer Keyser said, "you didn't stop him from doing it. You didn't make him put it back."

"I just didn't want to make a scene in the store."

"Kevin, because you didn't get Jeff to put the model back, you are an accomplice to the crime according to the laws of this state and will be treated the same way as Jeff. You could have said no."

"But he's my friend!"

"When you see your friend doing something wrong, you must not be afraid to speak up. If you can't say no, you shouldn't do things with kids who will get you into trouble."

Suddenly Kevin realized that he felt just like a criminal. His neck and hands became sweaty. *All because of a stupid model,* he thought.

"What will happen to us?" Jeff asked. "I'll be glad to pay for the model."

"It's too late for that." Officer Keyser opened his notebook. "Now, I need you, Mrs. Schrader, to give me certain routine information. I have to write out a citation, and I need to know such things as your son's full name, what school he attends, and how old he is."

In a halting voice, Jeff's mother answered all the questions. "Can we go now?" she asked, when Officer Keyser finished filling out the form.

"As soon as you sign it," he replied, "and I give you your copy. When you sign it, you agree to make sure your son shows up for his court date."

"Oh, my!" Mrs. Schrader exclaimed. "You mean he has to go to court?"

"I'm afraid so," Officer Keyser said. "Stealing is a crime."

"But he's only 11 years old. Can you do that?" She took a pen out of her purse and signed the citation.

"Yes," Officer Keyser said. "The way the state law reads, Jeff could be put on probation, have to pay a fine, or could even be put into a juvenile detention center. You can take him home now, but make sure he appears in court on July 23 at 2:00 P.M."

"Can I go now?" Jeff asked. "And what will happen to Kevin?"

"The same thing that is happening to you. He is an accomplice to your theft."

Jeff stood up stiffly and looked down at his friend. "I'm sorry, Kevin," he said slowly. "I didn't know that we would both get into trouble."

"I can't just let you kids come in here, steal things off the shelves, and get away every time," Mr. Mason said. "If I keep catching kids like you, maybe word will get out to all the kids."

Jeff hung his head as he walked out the door with his mother.

"OK," Officer Keyser said, turning to Kevin's father. "Now I need information from you."

As Kevin looked up at his father, a tear rolled down his cheek. "Dad, I'm sorry. Help me, please."

Mr. Walker put his arm around Kevin's shoulder before he turned to the policeman. "My son and I are ready to answer your questions," he said.

> He who walks with the wise grows wise, but a companion of fools suffers harm.
>
> Proverbs 13:20 NIV

Lord, help me stay away from kids who try to get me to do things I know are wrong. I don't want to get into trouble too, but sometimes I am tempted to go along with the crowd because it's easier. Help me to stand up for what I believe. Lead me to people who will help me become a stronger Christian.

Nobody's Perfect

"I saw Mrs. Hawkins at the grocery store," Mrs. Miller said. "She seemed pleased when I told her about the camp-out."

"You didn't invite Bobby, did you?" Gene asked.

"Yes. Why?"

"Because Mark, Sam, and I decided not to invite him."

"But you told me you were inviting all your neighborhood friends."

Gene frowned. "I wish you hadn't invited him, Mom. He'll just complain and make things miserable for everyone."

"It's too late to tell me now," Mrs. Miller said. "Besides, I don't think it's right to treat someone like that. Bobby has feelings too."

"But you don't know what it's like to listen to all his complaints," Gene said. "Today at school he complained that none of the baseball bats were right for him."

"What did the teacher do?"

"Made him use one." Gene walked partway down the hall. "Can't you call his mother and tell her you made a mistake?"

"No," Mrs. Miller replied. "He's already been invited."

On Saturday, after two days of packing and taking care of last-minute details, the four boys and Gene's parents piled into the car and headed for Gulch Lake State Park. "We'll be there pretty soon," Mr. Miller said.

"Will it be cold?" Bobby asked. "I don't like cold."

"Then why'd you come?" Gene asked. He saw his mother's look and stopped talking.

"It won't be that bad," Mark said. "The sleeping bags should keep us warm enough."

Half an hour later they pulled into the campground. "This is it, boys," said Mr. Miller. "Let's find a good spot to pitch the tents."

"Here's one," Sam called out a few minutes later. "It's pretty flat."

Gene walked over. "Yeah, it's good, and the hill will shelter us from the wind."

Mark laid a tent on the ground. "Let's put the door facing the hill." He and Gene unrolled the tent and staked down the corners.

"Why did you pick this spot?" Bobby said, dropping the hatchet. "That one over there looks better. You can see farther."

"It'll be dark in a while," Gene said. "We won't be able to see anything."

"I just thought it would be softer on the grass," Bobby stated.

The stake Gene was pounding hit a rock and bent. "Will you get me another stake, Bobby? It's on the tailgate."

As Bobby turned away, Gene motioned to the other boys. He lifted up the floor of the heavy canvas tent and slid in a flat rock. "Now he'll learn what a hard bed is like," Gene whispered. "We'll unroll his sleeping bag right on top of it."

"Serves him right for coming," Sam said. "He'll probably complain even if he catches six fish and no-body else catches any."

"If he does that," Mark said, "I'll throw him in."

"How's it going?" Mr. Miller walked up. "You've nearly got your tent up already! But you should probably tighten up the guy lines a little, Sam, in case the wind gets stronger in the night."

The boys set up both tents and walked over to where Mrs. Miller was cooking. "Dinner will be ready soon," she said. "I'm just waiting for the hamburgers to get done."

"I'm starving," Mark said, throwing a small stick on the fire. "They sure smell good."

"Hey, help me bring that bench over, will you?" Bobby looked at Gene.

"Why do you want it?" Gene asked.

"I want a place to sit down. It'll be more comfortable than this rock."

Gene started to say something, but his father nodded. "OK, I'll help," Gene said gruffly.

As soon as the hamburgers were cooked, everyone started eating. "This is a great dinner," Sam said. "Food always tastes better outside."

"The smoke gives the meat a nice taste," Mr. Miller said.

"Can somebody put mine on the fire again? It's too red in the middle. I like hamburgers well done."

Mr. Miller looked up, surprised. "Sure, Bobby. I'll do that for you."

Bobby swatted a mosquito. "Uh oh. The bugs are starting to come out."

"We've got plenty of bug repellant," Mrs. Miller answered.

"Anybody for throwing the Frisbee while we've still got light?" Gene asked. The boys walked over to a flat place where there weren't any trees.

"I'm glad we came here," Mark said. "I've never been here before. My parents always go to the Musikee River, and staying in a trailer just isn't the same as camping."

"I know what you mean," Sam agreed, throwing the Frisbee to Gene. "It'll be fun to fish tomorrow. I'll just put a grasshopper on my line and see what happens."

"You caught a big one last time we were here." Gene leaped into the air. "Hey, throw it a little lower, OK?" Then he deliberately threw the Frisbee way over Bobby's head and down a steep embankment.

"Where'd it go?" Bobby asked. "I don't see it."

"It's by the log." Sam watched Bobby hunt for the Frisbee.

"Maybe it's by the dead tree."

"No, it's in those weeds," Mark said.

The three boys moved closer together. "Let's hide behind those rocks," Sam said. "He'll never find us. Then we can play by ourselves and have some fun." They scurried behind the rocks and remained still.

Bobby finally found the Frisbee and walked back up.

"Hey, where are you?" he called out. "I found the Frisbee."

The boys didn't answer him.

"Come on, Gene," Bobby whined. "I want to play too."

"But we don't want you to play," Gene whispered, and Sam laughed quietly.

A moment later, Bobby walked back to the picnic table. "I can't find the guys."

"That's funny," Mr. Miller said, looking up from a magazine. "They were here just a second ago."

"Maybe they went down to the river," Mrs. Miller said. "Did you look there?"

"No." Bobby started walking down the road. As soon as he disappeared around a bend, the boys came out.

"What's for dessert?" Gene asked. "Can we make pies in the pie-maker?"

"A little later," his father answered. "Did you see Bobby? He's looking for you."

"We know," Gene said. "And he won't find us, either."

"You mean you deliberately hid from him?" Mrs. Miller exclaimed.

"Sorta," Gene answered, winking at Sam. "We just decided to let him be by himself for a while. We thought it would be good for him."

"I want to talk with you, Gene," Mr. Miller said. Gene followed his father to the car. "I'm only going to say this once, so listen carefully. Even if you didn't want Bobby to come along, he's here. You guys have to get along with him. I know he often complains, and I even get sick of hearing him sometimes." He paused. "But he does that because he wants attention and feels insecure. He can tell that you don't really want him along. If you keep this up, he'll be miserable."

"It's his fault," Gene responded.

"Not completely," his father answered. "You leave him out. You've got to love him, no matter how hard it is. I saw the look you gave him when he asked me to put his hamburger back on the fire."

"He's never satisfied with anything," Gene said. "He'd be OK if he didn't complain all the time. It's just no fun to be with somebody like that. He takes the joy out of doing things. We try to ignore him, but then he just complains more."

"Do you think if you included him he'd improve?" Mr. Miller asked. "Maybe he just wants to make sure you'll listen to what he says. Has he ever been camping before?"

"I don't know, Dad."

"Gene, I want you to be nice to him the rest of the time. Don't do anything more to bug him. Maybe we can help him realize that complaining is a bad habit."

"He won't change. Ever since he moved here he's been like that!" Gene put on his warm hat. "I came here to have fun, not to hear how bad things are or to get him to smile."

"I still expect you to be nice to him, and I want the other boys to be nice to him too. If you set a good example, maybe they'll follow it."

Just then Bobby appeared. "There you are. I've been looking all over for you."

As they ate dessert, Bobby asked, "What time will we get up? I didn't bring my alarm clock."

"When the sun comes up," Mr. Miller said.

"But can't I sleep in tomorrow?" Bobby asked.

Gene shot his father a look, as if to say, *See what I mean?*

"I think we'd better get to bed," Mr. Miller said. "We've got lots of things planned for tomorrow."

The boys climbed into the sleeping bags 15 minutes later. "Hey, this isn't so bad," Sam said. "I thought the ground would be a lot harder."

"It's always this hard, except when it rains." Mark shifted position.

"Get your feet out of my face," Gene said.

"Sorry." Mark moved back. "I didn't know your face was there."

"Man, my stomach is starting to hurt," Bobby said, "and I've got a rock in my back."

"You're always complaining," Gene said.

"No, I mean it. My stomach hurts. And there's a rock under here."

"Then I guess you'd better fix it."

"Can't you get it, Gene? You're closer to the door."

Gene thought for a second. "OK, I'll do it." The other boys were silent. *I bet they think I'm stupid,* Gene thought, *but maybe I can be nice to him for once.*

When Gene climbed back inside the tent after moving the rock, Bobby asked, "Could you close the tent flap, Sam? I've got chills. I can't get warm."

"Do it yourself," Sam said. "You're not helpless."

"I don't feel well," Bobby said. "All of a sudden my stomach hurts."

"Bobby," Mark said, "I'm tired and I want to sleep. Will you please quit complaining about everything and be quiet?"

The next morning, Gene got up first and fixed breakfast. Then he walked up next to the boys' tent. "Wake up. Breakfast is ready, and the fishing will be too good to miss."

"Give me a minute to find my glasses." Sam yawned. "I think they're in my boot. I can't wait to try my new lure in that one deep pool. I'll grab a donut and go on down to the river."

"Will you guys pipe down?" Bobby mumbled. "I didn't sleep much last night. My stomach hurt."

"Aren't you going fishing with us?" Gene asked.

"No. I don't think I can."

Sam and Mark stepped out of the tent. "You can sleep in there as long as you want," Mark said, "but we're going."

"I can't come. I don't feel well."

"Suit yourself," Mr. Miller said, walking up. "We'd like you to come if you want to."

Mr. Miller and the two boys quickly ate breakfast.

"I told you he wouldn't be any fun," Gene said as the three of them walked toward the river. "He's so used to complaining that he doesn't know how not to complain. And now he says he's sick so he can stay in bed."

"I still think it's important to help him realize how obnoxious his complaining is and be patient with him. But," Mr. Miller looked at the sun rising over the hills, "the fish won't wait for us all morning. Let's get down there and catch them. Mom promised to cook them after she wakes up."

Mark pointed. "There's Sam. He's already caught one!"

"This is going to be a good morning," Gene said.

The four of them fished along the bank for about

an hour, and everyone caught at least one trout. Suddenly they saw Mrs. Miller. "Come quickly," she called. "Bobby's really sick. I'm sure he has a fever."

"He did say he had chills last night," Gene said.

"What else did he say?" Mrs. Miller walked closer. "Why didn't you tell me?"

"I thought he was just complaining, as usual. He said he had a stomachache too."

"I'll go back with you," Mr. Miller said, laying down his pole.

"I guess he had a good reason to complain this time," Mark said. "It's too bad we didn't know he was telling the truth."

"We should have listened to him," Gene said. "I hope he isn't too sick."

> Love is very patient and kind, never . . . haughty or selfish or rude. Love does not demand its own way.
>
> 1 Corinthians 13:4 LB

You accept and love me just the way I am, Lord, but it's hard for me to love and accept people I don't like very much. Even though I know I'm not perfect, I sometimes try to make life miserable for people who do things I don't like. Help me become more sensitive to everyone I meet and to be willing to help them overcome bad habits. And make me willing to admit that I need other people's help too.

Timothy's Conscience

"How's it going?" the sixth grade teacher asked Timothy Franklin in the hallway. "You've been here a week, and you seem to fit in just fine."

"I like it," Timothy said slowly, "but it sure is different from my other school. The kids don't argue with their teachers as much here, and I left my ruler on my desk and nobody stole it."

Mrs. Mitchell chuckled. "I wasn't expecting that kind of an answer, but I guess you're probably right. The kids do take a lot of pride in the school. Are you all moved in?"

"Mostly," Timothy answered, "but I still have to help unpack some boxes."

"Don't let me delay you," Mrs. Mitchell said. "I just want you to know that I'm glad you're in my class."

"Thanks." Timothy's knapsack brimming with school books shifted from side to side as he hurried home. He turned down Cherry Street and couldn't help but look up at the tall oak trees. *I wonder what Phil and Tony would say if they were here?* he thought. *In Chicago we had to go to a park to see trees like this.* He slowed down. *But I miss the city and all my friends in the apartment building.*

A loud bark interrupted his thoughts, and he picked up a rock without even thinking about it. He was used to the stray dogs that ran in the alleys. *When I told Ken yesterday where I lived,* Timothy thought, *he warned me about an old lady's mean dog. He said it chased him down the street one day, and his mother called the police.* Timothy moved to the center of the street so he'd have more warning if the dog came.

After walking a block farther, Timothy saw a squirrel on a telephone wire and threw his rock at it. The rock just missed the squirrel and flew over the blossoming hedge. There was a bang, and then silence.

What did it hit? Timothy walked over to the hedge and peered through the branches. His rock lay on the hood of an older car in the driveway. *I hit the car!* He crouched down so nobody would see him. *I've got to get out of here before I get caught.* He looked both ways and then cut across the street. After he had gone a block, he started running.

Breathless, he opened the front door. "I'm home, Mom."

"How was school today?" His mother looked up from the couch. "How come you're out of breath?"

"I ran partway," Timothy answered quickly, feeling uncomfortable.

"Well, change your clothes. We need to move those boxes from the basement."

Timothy helped his sister and mother until they started dinner, and then he worked by himself. *I didn't mean to hit the car,* he thought. *It was an accident. I was only trying to hit the squirrel.* He began to worry that someone had followed him home after seeing him throw the rock.

During dinner his sister, Susan, kept giving him strange looks. Finally she asked, "Are you feeling OK? You sure are quiet."

"And you haven't eaten much," his father added. "You haven't even had seconds on potatoes."

"I'm all right," Timothy replied. "I'm tired. We played soccer in gym class."

Just then the telephone rang, and his mother picked up the receiver. Timothy stiffened. *Maybe they're calling to tell my parents what I did.* He sighed with relief when he figured out that it was just someone from Welcome Wagon who greeted families that moved into town.

After dinner he helped with the dishes and went to his room. But the harder he tried to study, the more difficult it was to keep his mind on his book. *I did see the rock on the hood of the car, but maybe it didn't dent anything,* he thought. *It was an older car, and they made cars stronger in those days.* He tried to remember if he had seen a dent, and all he could see was the rock perched on the hood. *It isn't my fault that the car was hidden behind that hedge. If I had seen it, I wouldn't have thrown the rock. And since nobody has telephoned, I guess I got away with it.*

"Timothy, would you like to come down and sample your sister's brownies?"

Startled, Timothy turned around. "I guess so. I didn't hear you knock."

"I didn't. Your door was open." His mother looked at him carefully. "Are you sure you're feeling all right?"

"I'm fine." Timothy forced a smile. "I'm tired."

"Well, you've been tired plenty of times before, and you haven't acted like this. Maybe the brownies will cheer you up."

"I put in extra nuts, just for you," Susan said as he entered the kitchen.

"Thanks." Timothy stuffed several brownies in his mouth and sat down in front of the television set.

"Are they good?" his sister asked, several minutes later.

"They're OK."

"Just OK? I thought they were your favorite, and Mom and I made them just for you."

"Cut it out, will you? I said they were OK, and I meant it. They're good."

Susan made a face. "You sure are crabby. That's the last time I'll make brownies for you."

"That's all right with me," Timothy said. "You can keep your brownies. I don't care."

He stood up and was halfway into the hall when his father said, "I'd like to talk with you for a minute, Timothy."

Timothy walked back into the room. His heart was beating quickly. *Does he know what happened?*

"I don't know what's eating you tonight," Mr. Franklin said, "but you sure are making everybody miserable. Would you mind telling me what's wrong?"

"I can't," Timothy said, squirming.

His father looked him in the eye. "I really don't

think your sister deserved the treatment you just gave her. She was only trying to cheer you up."

"I know. I didn't mean to say those things to her." Timothy walked into the kitchen. "I'm sorry, Susan. The brownies were really good, and I'm not just saying that."

Susan's face brightened. "I did the best I could. Mom's teaching me."

Timothy ate another one and started up the stairs. "I'm going to bed early."

"Good night," his mother called out. "I'd come up when you're ready for bed, but I've got to get this kitchen cleaned up and finish unpacking the good dishes. I'll wake you up tomorrow at 8:00. We have lots to do this weekend."

Timothy stuffed his face into the down pillow and tried to sleep. But he couldn't relax. He couldn't get the picture of the rock out of his mind. Finally he drifted into restless sleep and woke up in the middle of the night, sweating, after dreaming that somebody was chasing him.

When his mother came in the next morning, he was already awake. "I thought you were tired," she said.

"I was," Timothy yawned, "but I didn't sleep well. I had weird dreams."

"Your breakfast is on the table," his mother said, "and your father is already working in the garage. He'll need your help as soon as you're done."

After breakfast Timothy walked outside. His father was rearranging tools on a large sheet of pegboard. "Good morning, Timothy. Are you all rested?"

"Kinda." Timothy sat on a box. "I had a hard time sleeping." He paused. "Dad, have you ever had something happen that wasn't really your fault and yet it was?"

"I'm not sure what you mean," Mr. Franklin replied.

"Have you ever done something by accident and had to tell the person you did it?"

"Yes, I have." His father laid down the hammer. "I worked for a man while I was in high school to earn extra money. One afternoon I had to wash his car. His garage was really narrow, and when he drove the car in he left the wheels a little crooked. So when I backed out, I knocked some of the chrome off the side."

"What did you do then?" Timothy asked.

"Why, I had to tell him. It was hard, too, since he had a really nice car."

"Dad, could I leave for a while? I know you need my help, but I have something to do."

"I guess so. Is there something I can help you with?"

"Not this time." Timothy stood up. "I have to take care of this by myself."

"When will you be back?"

"As soon as I can."

Timothy walked back to where he had thrown the rock. *Why don't you just forget about the whole thing and quit making such a big deal out of it?* a small voice kept telling him. *You got away with it. Why go back now?*

He hesitated by the mailbox and then walked up the driveway. Suddenly a large German shepherd ran around the side of the house, barking fiercely. It was too late for Timothy to run, so he just stood there.

"What do you want?" an older woman asked, open-

ing her front door. "King, be still!" The dog stopped barking and eyed Timothy from about six feet away.

"Do you live here?" Timothy asked, feeling stupid because she probably did.

"Yes. What can I do for you? If you're selling candy for the school band, you're too late. I already bought two boxes, and I'm even allergic to chocolate."

"I'm not selling anything." Timothy's throat was dry. "I just came to talk to you about something."

"Come on in. You don't have to stand out there." The woman smiled. "King is really pretty friendly, once you get to know him. He just doesn't like strangers. Living alone and all, I'm glad I have him."

Not completely convinced, Timothy kept an eye on the dog as he walked to the door.

"Now what can I do for you?" the woman asked. "My name is Mrs. Randall."

"I'm Timothy," he blurted out, "and I hit your car with a rock yesterday. But I didn't mean to do it. I was only trying to hit a squirrel."

"Probably the one that gets into my bird feeder," the woman stated. "I saw the rock on there when I put the car into the garage last night. I thought another kid did it."

"What other kid?"

"One boy teases the dog by throwing rocks at him from the other side of the hedge. He even put big rocks on my driveway and then called the police when King chased him away."

"I didn't mean to hit your car," Timothy said.

"I'm sure you didn't," the woman said. "It did scratch the hood, though."

"Last night," Timothy said, "I kept trying to forget that I threw it, but I couldn't."

"So you came here to make things right?"

Timothy nodded. "But I don't have much money."

"Well, I tell you what. Let's go out and look at the scratch. If it's something I should have fixed, then maybe we can work out a deal. Maybe you can help me in the garden or something."

"I like to work outside. In Chicago we didn't even have a yard."

As they walked out the back door, King brushed against Timothy's right leg. *So this is the mean dog Ken was telling me about,* he thought. *A new guy has a lot to learn. Ken should have been more friendly.* Timothy felt himself smiling. He couldn't wait to get home.

> What happiness for those whose guilt has been forgiven! What joys when sins are covered over! What relief for those who have confessed their sins and God has cleared their record.
>
> Psalm 32:1 LB

Lord, when I do something wrong I feel guilty, even if I don't get caught. Help me to be able to tell the person I've wronged that I'm sorry. Thank you for forgiving me when I confess what I've done. It feels so good to be forgiven.

But My Best Isn't Good Enough

Mr. Turner held up his hand. "On your mark, get set, go!" Six boys and girls dashed toward the finish line, their classmates cheering them on.

Tony turned to Lance. "We're not going to beat Miss Stockwell's class unless we do a lot better."

Lance nodded. "Yeah, when Mr. Turner suggested that we compete against the other fifth grade class, I thought it was a dumb idea. But it's fun." He looked across the field where his twin sister was cheering for her class. "Jennifer is really going to be hoarse to-night. I hope we beat them."

"Are you ready to go?" Tony asked. "It's our turn next."

"I guess so." Lance shaded his eyes against the sun. "It looks like Pete and Larry crossed the line in first and second place. That means we're about tied." He rolled up his shirt sleeves.

"All right," Mr. Turner said. "This is the last event. Are you ready to start?"

Lance's sister hurried over. "How far do we have to go?"

"Down to where Miss Stockwell is standing and back. Do you all understand how to run a wheelbarrow race?"

"Yeah," Jennifer said. "We've done it before."

"Do we have to go all the way across the finish line to win or just have an arm across it?" Tony asked.

"You both have to cross it completely," Mr. Turner replied.

The two groups of students eyed each other. "We don't want your class to win," one boy said. "We'll never hear the end of it."

"It's no big deal," a girl on the other team responded. "There's no prize."

Four students from each class walked to the line, and Lance grabbed Tony's ankles. "Come on, Tony," a girl with glasses shouted when the whistle blew. "You can do it! Hurry up, Larry."

"Faster," another girl yelled. "They're gaining on you!" Lance walked as fast as Tony could go.

Walking on your hands isn't easy, Lance thought. *I'm glad Tony has strong arms.* He looked over to see how his sister was doing. *She's way ahead.* He took larger steps, forcing Tony to go faster.

"Hey, my arms aren't *that* long." Tony dropped down on one shoulder. "Don't go so fast."

"Sorry," Lance said.

"Hurry up," Tim shouted, "you guys have to do well." Lance and Tony went across the chalk line near Miss Stockwell and started back.

"We're doing all right," Lance said. "Even if Larry

and Mike come in second and we come in third, our class will win." He turned to look at how his sister was doing and tripped. Both he and Tony fell in a heap and started laughing. By the time they untangled themselves, the other three pairs were way ahead. A minute later, they crossed the finish line in last place.

"We lost because of you guys," Paul said, walking over to Lance and Tony. "Why'd you have to fall down?"

"Yeah," another boy said. "We'd have won if it weren't for you. Larry and Mike came in second."

"I'm glad you're so great," Tony replied. "Maybe everyone should be like you."

"We sure did better than you did," Paul said. "He and I came in first in our races." He walked closer to Lance. "Maybe if you didn't trip over your own feet, you'd do better." Lance didn't answer; he just looked the other way.

"You didn't have to say that," Tony said. "Who do you think you are, anyway? The greatest athlete in the world?"

The school bell rang, and Mr. Turner blew his whistle. "That's it. Miss Stockwell's class won by two points." Several girls cheered.

Lance walked slowly toward the gym. "Hey, I heard what Paul said to you." A short boy came up beside Lance. "Don't let it bother you. He thinks he's the greatest, and he has to prove it to everybody."

"Maybe he's right," Lance muttered. "I do trip over my own feet."

"Nobody's perfect," the boy said. "Besides, you're the best reader in the class."

"Being good in English doesn't win races." Lance

50

yanked open the door. "I let our class down. But thanks anyway."

Later that afternoon, as Lance entered the living room, his sister greeted him with, "What did you think about the race today? Did you see how fast I went?"

"Yeah."

"How'd you do, Lance?" their brother, Gary, asked.

"He fell down," Jennifer said. "But Anne and I made it all the way without falling, so my class won."

"I asked Lance," Gary said.

"She's right. My class was doing pretty well until I tripped." Lance felt discouraged. "As usual, she did better than I did."

"You can't help it if you're uncoordinated," Jennifer said.

"Jennifer, that wasn't a nice thing to say." Mrs. Stone entered the room.

"I wasn't trying to be mean," Jennifer countered. "It's true. It isn't his fault."

Lance hurried out of the room. *She's right,* he thought. *I'm not good in sports. Even in a wheelbarrow race, something happens. Why can't I be like Tony? He can do everything.* Lance looked down at his skinny legs. *I'll never be that good.*

"Can I come in?" Gary asked.

"Yeah."

"I just wanted to tell you something," Gary said. "I know how you feel. I know what it's like to try your hardest and still blow it."

"How could you know?" Lance retorted. "You're on the first-string basketball team, and you do well in track too."

"But did you ever stop to think that I was once

51

your age?" Gary asked. "I used to be just like you. I could never hit a baseball, and every time I threw a football it wobbled. I even dribbled a basketball high so I wouldn't lose control of it, and then people stole it away from me."

Lance looked up. "So what'd you do?"

"I felt sorry for myself at first, and I was jealous of the other guys. But then the gym teacher helped me realize that my body was growing so fast that I couldn't expect to be coordinated all at once. And I gave myself time to improve."

"But what if I don't improve? I may not be like you when I get bigger."

Gary laughed. "I'm sure you won't be just like me. You're already taller than I was at your age." He paused. "There's a lot more to life than being good at sports. You're good in other things, a lot better than I'll ever be."

"Like what?"

"Like repairing your bicycle," Gary answered. "But you're never going to make it if you keep feeling sorry for yourself. You've got to use the talents you've been given and be thankful for who you are. You have to be patient with yourself."

"But people laugh at me," Lance protested.

"So what? If you're doing your best, that's what counts. Sometimes it seems like it, but winning isn't everything. There will always be another chance to do better. Just keep believing in yourself. You've got a lot of things going for you."

Lance stood up. "Sometime could you play basketball with me and teach me some things?"

"How about after dinner tonight?" Gary asked.

"I'll show you some neat moves, and I won't laugh at you. I promise."

"You better not," Lance said, grinning.

> God has given each of us the
> ability to do certain things well.
> Romans 12:6 LB

Sometimes I want to win so badly, Lord, and yet no matter how hard I try I still lose. It's not my fault that my body is growing so fast, and yet I feel like there's something wrong with me. Help me to learn that you created me with special gifts. Maybe I won't ever be great in sports, but I want to become the person you want me to become. And if that means losing sometimes, help me to accept that.

Stephen's Difficult Decision

Mr. Yancey erased the chalkboard and turned to the seven boys in his Sunday school class. "Before the bell rings, I want to know how many of you would be interested in a weekend bicycle trip. We'd leave on a Friday and come home on a Sunday night."

"Then we'll miss church," Stephen said.

"Not exactly," Mr. Yancey replied, "because we'll have a Bible and prayer time wherever we are. And I'll make sure you all do your Sunday school lessons too."

"But you won't have a chalkboard to draw pictures on," Douglas said.

"Maybe," Larry said, grinning, "we could take some chalk and camp near a sidewalk."

"That's enough." Mr. Yancey looked at his watch. "First we have to decide if you guys want to go. If you do, you'll need permission from your parents."

"Where would we go?" Paul, a thin boy with dark hair, asked.

"I think Osage State Park would be a nice place," Mr. Yancey said. "The Canyon Reservoir Wilderness area is a possibility, but it's nicer in the spring."

"I don't know if I could ride that far," Stephen remarked. He stood up and limped around the room. "Oh, my aching legs, oh, my aching legs."

"You'll make it," Al said. "You deliver all those newspapers every day using your bicycle."

"How about you, Randy?" Mr. Yancey asked. "Want to go?"

"I guess so. It sounds like fun."

"What about the rest of you?"

"I think it's a good idea," Al said, looking around at everyone. "But wouldn't a trip like that cost a lot of money?"

"Not as much as you'd think," Mr. Yancey answered. "I've worked out a way for you to earn the money you'll need. If all of you show up at the church on Saturday morning about 9:00, you can help the church custodian with the fall yard work."

"I can't," Tom stated suddenly. "I have to help my father on Saturday. He's starting a new business."

"What do you do for him?" Stephen asked.

"That doesn't matter," Mr. Yancey said. "If he can't come on Saturday, he can't come. We'll work something else out. Before our time is up, listen carefully. Here are the permission slips for the trip. We'll leave a week from Friday. I need this slip back from each of you, signed by your parents, at the end of this week. Bring it with you on Saturday or Sunday." Each boy took a slip.

"I'm glad we're doing this now," Al said. "If we waited much longer, it'd be too cold."

"How'll we keep warm?" Randy asked. "I get cold easily."

"I have several extra sleeping bags if you don't have one," Mr. Yancey said. "My wife can drive all our gear to the campsite ahead of time so we won't have to carry it all."

"Wouldn't that be cheating?" Tony asked. "If we're going to bike camp, we shouldn't take a car too."

"Well, then we'll have to take less stuff," Mr. Yancey said. "My brother has a special trailer that hooks up to a bicycle. Hey, it's nearly time for church." The boys stacked their chairs against the wall.

"Don't you want to earn money for the trip?" Stephen asked Tom as they walked out the door.

"Yes, but I promised Dad I'd help him."

"Can't you get out of it?"

"No. I promised." Tom stared at Stephen. "It's too late to change plans. Besides, he needs me." When the boys reached the sanctuary, they split up.

On Saturday, Mr. Yancey showed up to help the boys. "Has anybody talked with Tom to see if he's going camping with us?"

"I wonder if he really wants to come," Stephen said. "When I mentioned it at school yesterday, he said he'd rather stay home and work."

"Are you sure?" Al asked, piling up the leaves. "He's a fun guy to have along."

"I'll phone him tonight," Mr. Yancey said.

Later that evening, Mr. Yancey called Tom. "Can you come with us next weekend? Everyone else is going, and they were asking about you today."

"They were?" Tom paused. "I'd like to go, but I can't."

"Why not?"

"I . . . don't have a bicycle. Mine was stolen. But Dad is going to help me buy a new one once the business gets going."

"Why didn't you say that in the first place?" Mr. Yancey asked. "I don't have an extra bicycle, but maybe one of the other boys does."

"I didn't want to be a bother."

The next morning, everyone showed up for Sunday school but Tom. "Where is he?" Stephen asked. "Doesn't he want to know the plans?"

Mr. Yancey explained Tom's problem. "He doesn't want to ask anyone to lend him a bicycle."

"I don't have one to lend," Al stated, "and my brother sure wouldn't let anyone use his." One by one the boys told Mr. Yancey that they didn't have an extra bicycle.

"It's too bad." Mr. Yancey shook his head. "I really want Tom to be able to go with us. Maybe I'll rent one for him."

That afternoon, Stephen sat down in his room. *I don't have an extra bike to lend Tom today,* he thought. *I won't get my new bike until Wednesday, and I don't want to lend that to anyone.* He smiled as he thought about the ten-speed his parents had ordered for his birthday. *It'll sure be better than that old three-speed I've had since I was eight.* He walked outside and looked at his old bike. *I could lend this one to Tom,* he thought. But the longer Stephen looked at the old bike, the more he realized that it would be too small for Tom. *He's way taller than I am, and this bike is nearly too small for me.*

Stephen walked to the end of the driveway. *But what if something happens to my new bike? On our last camping trip, Tom got the zipper on the tent all jammed.*

Finally Stephen telephoned Tom. "Hey, if you want to go with us," he said, choosing his words carefully, "and you don't have to work, I could lend you a bike."

"What'll you ride?" Tom replied. "You don't have two bikes, do you?"

"Not now, but my new ten-speed gets here on Wednesday. I'll ride my old one because it'd be too small for you."

"Are you sure you want to do that, Stephen?" Tom exclaimed.

Stephen suddenly realized he really did mean it. "That's what friends are for."

"It's hard for me to accept, but I will anyway," Tom said. "I'd hate to miss the trip. Our class has lots of fun."

"You're right," Stephen agreed.

"As soon as Dad's business gets going," Tom said, "he's buying me a ten-speed too."

"Next week, Osage State Park," Stephen declared. "Next spring, the Canyon Reservoir Wilderness area."

> Don't forget to do good and to share what you have with those in need.
>
> Hebrews 13:16 LB

Lord, I know I'm not supposed to be selfish, but sometimes I want my things all to myself. Help me to share in a responsible way so that what you have given me won't be needlessly ruined. Thank you for the joy I receive when I help someone else. Make me willing to ask for help when I need it.

Who's Afraid of a Little Wind?

Ken hopped from rock to rock on the water's edge. Being careful not to get his feet wet as the whitecaps broke on the shore, he leaned down and picked up a piece of driftwood.

"There's a lot of driftwood around here."

Startled, Ken turned around. A tanned boy was sitting on an overturned rowboat. "Hi," Ken said. "I didn't see you."

"I saw you coming down the beach as I was going to our pier." The boy shook sand out of his left shoe. "I'm getting ready to go sailing. This wind'll be great."

"You've got a boat?" Ken asked. "I've always wanted to go sailing, but we live in Iowa."

"I've never been there, but I've heard it's hot and flat," the boy said. "I knew you weren't from around here. Your arms are too white."

Ken looked down at his arms. "I'll get brown.

63

We're going to be here for three weeks." He looked out across the water. "Do you sail often?"

"My dad lets me take the boat out whenever I want to," the boy said proudly. "My name's David. What's yours?"

"Ken."

"Are you renting that cottage in Miller's Cove?"

Ken nodded. "Yeah. We just got here yesterday."

David pulled his cap down tighter on his head. "I've been waiting all week for a wind like this. It's no fun going sailing when the wind isn't strong."

"It seems almost too windy to me." Ken put his hands in his pockets.

"After you've been sailing as much as I have, you'll understand what I mean." David walked to the pier, with Ken trailing along behind. "Want to see my boat?"

"Sure." Ken followed David down the wooden pier. "Hey, the boat has a place to crawl inside."

"That's the cockpit," David said. "It doesn't hold much, but it comes in handy."

"How many passengers can the boat carry?"

"Three or four," David replied. "It's really fast."

"Can I go out with you?" Ken asked cautiously. "I'll keep out of the way."

"I don't see why not. But I'm ready to leave now."

"I'll be right back," Ken said quickly. "I'm just going to run back and get a jacket." He ran down the pier, across the beach, and up the wooden steps to the cottage.

"Where've you been?" his father asked, laying down his newspaper.

"On the beach." Ken dashed into the bedroom.

"What's the hurry?"

"I just met a boy about my age, and he invited me to go sailing with him. Can I go?" Ken's voice wavered. "I've wanted to go sailing for a long time."

"I think you should wait until we rent a boat at the harbor," Mr. Jamison said, looking out the large picture window. "Sailing can be lots of fun, but today isn't a good day for sailing. It's too gusty."

"Aw, Dad, he knows a lot about sailing. He lives here all year."

"I still don't think it's a good idea. There will be a better day, I'm sure. Besides," he added, "how do you know the boy really knows how to sail?"

Ken sighed. "Then what'll I do? I get bored just walking along the beach."

"There's a lot to see on the beach, if you'd just be observant," his mother stated. "You could probably find a crab and some starfish, not to mention some pretty shells."

"I don't want to hunt for shells," Ken said.

"You could always read. You brought lots of books."

"I don't want to read either."

"Your mother and I are going into town in an hour or so. Want to come?"

"I guess so." Ken pushed the screen door open and watched the gray clouds swirl. *I think it's a good day for sailing,* he thought. *Who's afraid of a little wind?*

"All set?" David asked impatiently when Ken walked onto the pier. "I've been waiting for you."

"Sorry. I had to work out some things with my parents." Ken stopped at the end of the pier and watched the curling waves sweep under his feet. "I can't go with you now."

"Why not?"

"My father doesn't think it's a good day."

"Did he say you couldn't go?" David looked up.

Ken thought for a minute. "He didn't specifically tell me I couldn't go, but I know what he meant."

"Maybe you misunderstood him." David pointed. "Untie that rope, will you?"

Ken walked over to the boat and knelt down. "Dad says it's too rough today."

"What does he know about sailing? Does he have a sailboat?"

"He doesn't own a boat," Ken answered, "but he used to sail with friends."

"Then don't worry about it," David stated confidently. "He doesn't know this area like I do." A large wave dashed against one of the posts and splashed the boys. "You don't want to get out there and just sit in one place, do you? That's no fun."

"No," Ken said hesitantly, looking back at the cottage. "At least I don't think I do. But I still think I should wait and go with you another time."

"Who says we'll get another wind like this while you're here? It's now or never. If you don't want to go, I guess I'll go by myself."

"I do want to go," Ken replied, "but—"

"Then undo that rope and climb in." David stuffed two life jackets into the cockpit. "We have to have these in the boat, or we can be fined. But we don't have to wear them."

"Give me one," Ken said. "I don't swim very well."

"You won't need it today, and it's already packed." David gave Ken a funny look. "Only sissies wear them."

"All right, I won't wear it, but hand it to me anyway."

David tossed him the life preserver and pushed

the boat away from the pier. "Just hold onto the side of the boat and let me do the rest." When David raised the sails, they began to flap. "Lower the centerboard, Ken. It's deep enough here."

"What's a centerboard?"

"This thing." David pointed. "Pull it toward you and it'll go down."

"What does it do?"

"It helps to keep the boat from drifting sideways, and sometimes," David said, grinning, "it catches seaweed in shallow water." He passed a line through a cleat and put his right hand on the rudder.

"We're moving!" Ken exclaimed, watching the water swirl past the end of the boat.

"I told you this boat was fast," David bragged.

"We won't stay out too long, will we?" Ken sat on a cushion. "I have to be back in an hour. My parents are going into town."

"You'll be back in time."

A large wave smacked into the boat; water splashed over the sides. "Whew, that water's cold."

"You'll get used to it," David said. "After a while you—" A gust of wind suddenly hit the sails. The boat heeled over precariously, and water started coming in. "Move over to the other side of the boat," David shouted.

Ken crawled over the centerboard and under the boom so quickly that he banged his knee. "Next time give me more warning."

"I'll try," David said. "See that plastic bucket? We have to bail the water out before it goes into the cockpit."

Ken grabbed the bucket. "Why'd the boat slant so much?"

David frowned. "Who's doing the sailing, you or me? It's not my fault this wind is so strong."

"I thought you said that it's good to sail when the wind is like this," Ken replied.

"I did," David said, licking the salt spray off his lips. "But this wind is stronger than I thought."

Suddenly the boom spun across the hull, nearly knocking Ken out of the boat and bruising his shoulder. Getting up, Ken saw David struggling to get the line out of the cleat to loosen the sail. "You said you were a good sailor and you do this all the time," Ken said as the boat once again headed into the waves.

"I do go out sometimes," David said defensively. "I've just never gone out this far before."

"How long have you had this boat?" Ken asked.

"My father bought it this spring." David tightened his grip on the rudder. "Man, we're really moving now."

The breeze cut through Ken's jacket; he began to shiver but didn't say anything about it.

As the boat chopped into the whitecaps, water sprayed over the bow. "Isn't this fun?" David said. "Look at the big wave coming up."

The clouds were thicker now, and Ken turned around. The cottage looked small and desolate. "Don't you think we've gone far enough?" he asked, watching the dark water swirl by.

"We'll turn back soon," David said. The boat began to pitch up and down as the waves grew larger. "Now I'll show you how well this boat can turn. We're going to come about. When I tell you, you'll have to move quickly to the other side." David pulled the rudder toward him. "OK, now move!" The sailboat

turned suddenly just as another gust of wind hit the sails. The boom hit Ken on the shoulder and knocked him backwards.

"Get to the other side," David yelled as a large wave hit them broadside. Freezing cold water poured into the boat and ran into the cockpit. Ken fell overboard and came up gasping for air. David climbed up as high as he could on the opposite side, trying to raise the sails out of the water. Seconds later, the mast began sinking.

"Climb on," David screamed, and Ken grabbed hold of the mast.

"Not that way. Swim to where I am and climb up on the centerboard."

"I can't," Ken yelled, just before he was buried in a wave. He drew another breath, his eyes wide with fear. "I can't swim that well."

David slid off the side of the boat into the water too.

Ken clung to the mast, trying to keep from being bruised as the waves pounded against the boat. The cold water numbed him; his clothing weighted him down. The mast and sails sank lower, and he grabbed hold of the rudder. When the boat turned completely over, the rudder cut into Ken's hand and he lost his grip. "What do I hold onto?" he shouted. "My life jacket is gone." David didn't answer. He was trying desperately to hold onto the slippery edge of the boat.

The boys clung to the hull as it bobbed up and down. The waves kept knocking their hands loose, and Ken's arms felt like they were made of lead. He began to shiver uncontrollably.

"Hold on!" someone shouted, and Ken thought he heard a motor. A moment later, his father pulled him into a large boat. He hunched over in the seat to escape the biting wind. Soon David sat dripping beside him.

"What'll my dad say when he gets home?" David said, his lips blue. "I wasn't supposed to take the boat out by myself."

I sure was wrong about David, Ken thought, gratefully accepting the cup of hot tea that was handed him. A large lump formed in his throat when his father wrapped him in a blanket and put an arm around his shoulders. "I'm sorry," Ken said, his teeth clenched.

"You're lucky," his father said. "If I hadn't seen you on the boat and seen the boat in trouble, and if the neighbor hadn't been home, you'd still be hanging on."

A wise son heeds his father's instruction.

Proverbs 13:1 NIV

Lord, I really enjoy sports like sailing and baseball, and I thank you for the rules that make them fun. Help me to obey the rules and to avoid taking risks just because a friend wants me to. Thank you for people who care enough about me to not let me do dangerous things.

Boy, Are You Lucky!

Michael Springer opened up a roll of pennies and dumped them onto the living room rug just as his mother walked in. "How are you doing?" she asked. "Find any good ones?"

"Not yet," Michael said, "but I still have 10 more rolls to look through."

"Dad and I are going shopping this afternoon. Need any coin books?"

"No. I have a hard enough time filling the ones I have," Michael said, carefully examining each penny. A few minutes later he heard the car start.

He opened roll after roll of coins and found several pennies that were in better shape than the ones he had. *I wonder if Roger found any while he was visiting his dad in Boston?* he thought. *Right now I have some he doesn't have, and he's been collecting a lot longer than I have.*

Suddenly he gasped. *I finally found a 1932P!* he

thought. *I thought I'd never get one.* He held the penny up to the light of the tall floor lamp. *Even Roger doesn't have this. Wait'll I show it to him!*

The clock struck three as Michael finished looking through the coins. He counted out piles of 50 and refilled each paper tube. *Roger's plane was supposed to get in at two,* Michael thought, *so he's probably home by now.* He stood up and pulled on his tennis shoes. Putting his coin books in a bag, he headed out the front door and over to Roger's.

"Hi, Mrs. Watson. Is Roger back yet?"

Mrs. Watson smiled. "He's unpacking. Come in." Then she called upstairs. "Michael's here."

"Send him up," Roger answered.

"So how was your trip?" Michael asked, stepping into Roger's room.

"Great. Dad drove me to a big coin show and a coin store." Roger opened up a drawer. "Look at these. Dad gave me money for them."

"You should see what I have." Michael opened his bag. "I found a 1932P penny."

"I got one too!" Roger opened an envelope. "It's in very good to fine shape. I bought it at the coin store."

"Yours is better than mine," Michael said, his voice heavy with disappointment. "You're lucky. I wish my father would buy me coins. I looked through twenty rolls today before I found this, and I've been looking for it for months."

"Yeah, it's a lot easier to buy them, but it isn't as much fun. Want to see the other coins I got?"

"No thanks," Michael said, standing up. "I've gotta get going."

"But you just got here, and it won't take long. Look at this dime!"

Michael grew more upset. "I really don't want to see your coins," he declared.

Roger looked hurt. "Why do you say that? I'd like to see yours."

"Look at those." Michael pointed to the coins in the drawer. "I probably could never find those looking through rolls I get from the bank, and your dad just buys them for you."

"At least you get to look through them with your father sometimes," Roger blurted out. "I only get to see my father twice a year, and this time he just gave me the money to buy coins and didn't even go in with me. I'd rather have my father here than all the coins in the world." He slammed the drawer shut.

It was stupid, Michael thought, *for me to feel that way. How did I know Roger's father just gave him the money and didn't care enough to go with him to buy the coins?*

"Michael, your father is on the phone."

"Thanks, Mrs. Watson."

"You can take it up there if you want to."

Michael entered the hallway and picked up the receiver. "Hello, Dad."

"I just found out," Mr. Springer said, "that Mr. Swanson's son collects coins and wants to do some trading. Shall we go over after supper and take your duplicates?"

"You bet," Michael said. "Can Roger go too?"

"Yes, that would make it even better."

Michael turned to his friend. "My dad wants to know if you want to go with us tonight to do some trading."

76

"I'll ask Mom," Roger said. "I've been hoping I could trade my 1950D nickel for some of the pennies I still need." He paused. "I'm sorry I said those things to you."

"I'm sorry too." Michael smiled. "All of a sudden I felt jealous, like I was competing to get more coins than you or something."

"We're both lucky," Roger said. "Let's just be friends, OK? Coins aren't worth fighting over."

Michael nodded his head in agreement and walked back to the telephone. "Dad, he wants to come, but he has to ask his mother."

"Fine," Mr. Springer said. "Let me know at dinner."

Roger and Michael then hurried downstairs.

> Beware! Don't always be wishing for what you don't have.
>
> Luke 12:15 LB

Lord, so many people want more things, even though they already have so much to be thankful for. Help me to be satisfied with what I have and not to be jealous when one of my friends gets something I'd like. And teach me to really appreciate the people in my life who are special to me.

You Broke It!

"Hey, Mom, can I sleep over at Todd's tomorrow night?" Nine-year-old Allen ran upstairs from the basement.

"That sounds fine," Mrs. Renault said. "Tonight Susan will be coming over. She said she wouldn't mind staying here a few hours while we're at Campbell's."

"She wouldn't mind baby-sitting, you mean." Karen walked into the room. "She's just coming over to make sure we act OK."

"That's not the only reason," her mother said, "but it's part of the reason. She thought it would be nice to spend time in a house and get out of her apartment for a while." She looked out the window. "Dad's ready, and we're late. See you later."

Allen watched the car's lights disappear around the corner. Then he went into the living room to read.

"What're you reading?" Karen asked, sitting down on the couch. "Some book about baseball, I suppose."

"No. I'm reading about how some boys solve a mystery." Allen ate another cookie.

"Why don't you read about girls solving a mystery?"

" 'Cause this book isn't about girls." Allen continued reading. "Hey, why'd you throw that pillow at me?"

"I felt like it," Karen said. "You think all girls are dumb."

"I'm going to think it more if you don't cut it out." Allen rolled over. "Go talk on the telephone. You're good at doing that."

"I don't want to."

"Then do something. Quit staring at me—you look so weird."

"I do, do I? Speak for yourself." She threw another pillow at him, harder this time, and it knocked several cookies off the paper plate.

"Look what you did to the cookies!"

"You shouldn't eat them anyway." Karen pointed to his stomach. "Mom keeps telling you not to eat so much, but you won't listen."

"I don't eat that much," Allen answered, "and I'm no fatter than you." He threw a pillow at her head; it bounced off the edge of the couch and hit a picture.

"Now look at what you did," Karen said. "The picture's crooked. You're lucky you didn't knock it off the wall."

"If you hadn't moved, I wouldn't have hit it."

"You think you're so cool." Karen kicked his book. It slid across the rug.

"That's not mine," Allen yelled, jumping up. "And you kicked it."

"So what if I did?" Karen picked up another pillow. "You weren't reading it anyway."

"How could I, with you bothering me?" Allen's face began to turn red. "Why don't you just shut up and let me be?"

"You sure are friendly tonight." Karen's voice trailed off as she stepped into the family room. "I'm going to watch television."

"No you're not," Allen stated. "My show starts soon, and Mom said I could watch it."

"She's not here, so who cares? I'll get there first."

Allen ran after her. As he grabbed at her arm, she shoved him toward a table. His elbow hit a lamp, and it crashed to the floor.

"Look, you broke it!" Karen yelled.

"What do you mean? It wasn't my fault. You pushed me."

The doorbell rang. "Look what you did," Karen repeated, "and Susan's here now. What will she do when she sees it?"

For the rest of the evening, after both Allen and Karen refused to clean up the broken lamp, Allen stayed in his room. *Why'd she push me?* he thought. As he sat at his desk, he heard broken pieces clinking together. *I guess Susan decided to clean it up.*

The next morning, Allen sat down at the kitchen table. "What happened last night?" Mr. Renault asked sternly. "Susan said that when she got here, the lamp was in pieces and you both refused to clean up the mess."

"He chased me," Karen said quickly.

"Why did he do that?" Mr. Renault asked.

"I don't know," Karen replied in an innocent voice.

"She wouldn't let me read my book." Allen looked up at his father. "She kept bothering me and throwing pillows at me. Then she said she was going to turn on the television so I couldn't watch my program. It wasn't my fault the lamp broke."

"Well then, it seems the lamp just fell off the table by itself, huh?" Mr. Renault looked at Allen and then at Karen. "Just after we leave the house, the lamp decides to fall off the table."

"That's not funny, dear," Mrs. Renault said quietly.

"I'm not amused either." Mr. Renault's voice rose. "I'm really tired of your excuses. Who broke the lamp?"

"She did!" Allen exclaimed.

"He did," Karen said.

"As far as I can tell, you both broke it, so in that sense you both are guilty. Now tell us what happened." Mrs. Renault shook her head. "Blaming one another won't put the lamp back together."

"I didn't mean to knock it off the table," Allen said, "and I'm sorry. I was chasing her and she pushed me."

"I didn't mean to push Allen that hard," Karen said. "It was an accident, and I'm sorry I teased him."

"How do you feel about breaking the lamp?" her mother asked.

"Oh, I'm sorry about that too." Karen thought for a minute. "I even tried to think of a way to help buy a new one, but I couldn't. I'm too young to baby-sit or clean for people. But I might be able to wash the neighbors' windows." Her face brightened.

"And I could shovel driveways," Allen added.

"I know you'd like to help pay for the lamp," Mr. Renault said, "but I'm afraid that it would take you a long time to do that. The lamp can be replaced, but it was expensive." The children's smiles faded. "But," he added, "I think Mom and I have a clearer understanding of what happened. If you promise not to roughhouse inside, I think we can work something out."

Both Karen and Allen agreed that they'd try to do better.

"Instead of severely punishing you for what happened," Mrs. Renault continued, "we've decided to take you with us when we buy things to use in redecorating the family room. When you learn how much well-made things cost, you'll be more careful with them. And," she added, "we want to include you in the decorating too. You can help hang a picture, learn to arrange things on a shelf, and put books in a bookcase. But no complaining if you miss an activity once in a while, OK?"

Karen and Allen looked at each other. "OK," Allen said.

"We like having a nice home too," Karen added.

> Tell the truth. Be fair. Live at peace with everyone.
> Zechariah 8:16 LB

Help me, Lord, to admit when I've done something wrong and to make things right again. Brothers and sisters can be mean sometimes, and often I get into trouble when I lose my temper. Give me more patience so I can avoid quarrels. Thank you for answering this prayer.

Bill Runs Away

"How come the driveway isn't shoveled?" Mrs. Pike asked, dropping her purse on the faded sofa. "Didn't I tell you to do that as soon as you got home from school?"

"I just got home," Bill replied. "I stayed after school to ask Mr. Hanson, the special science teacher, how birds know when to migrate. Then I caught the last bus."

"I'm getting tired of this, day after day," Mrs. Pike complained. "I work at the restaurant to earn money so we can eat and pay the heating bills, and then I have to order you to do your chores. Why can't you just do as you're told?"

"Mother," Bill said, "Mr. Hanson told me today he'd be glad to answer any questions I have, but I can't talk with him until my last class is over."

"It's not right," his mother said. "Why don't you

ask your own teacher and get home on time? Isn't she smart enough for you?"

"I do ask her," Bill answered, "but she won't look up things she doesn't know. I asked her last week how bees live through the cold winter, and she told me to come back another time. Then, on Wednesday, I asked why geese fly in V-shaped formations, and she laughed and told me it was because all but the front one were nearsighted."

"I'm not surprised that she laughed," Mrs. Pike said. "Kids today need to learn how to work hard, instead of learning about things that don't really matter. Geese won't buy your lunch at school every day."

"I work pretty hard," Bill said, "and I help you out a lot, much more than when Dad was home."

"From now on," Mrs. Pike said, "I want you to come right home after school. If you think you have a lot of work, think again. Now that your sister is married, you're the only one left. As soon as you are old enough to get a real job and leave home, out you go." She sighed and turned up the volume on the television set. "I don't see what good school does. Good jobs are too hard to find."

"Things are different now. If I go to college, I'm going to get a good job."

"So you think you're going to college?" His mother shrugged her shoulders. "Maybe you think the money will drop into our laps?"

"No, I don't. But some schools give scholarships."

"They're only for smart people who know how to work. And you don't even empty the garbage. The whole kitchen smells, and I refuse to do it. It's your job."

"I'll do it," Bill said. "Just let me take my books up to my room."

"Don't ask me any more of those silly questions, either. Just because I don't know the answers doesn't mean I don't know anything." His mother pointed to a picture hung over the sofa. "I've got talent. I just don't have time to paint right now."

"It's a good painting," Bill said, wishing he could wipe all the dust off the frame.

"I got my education from the school of life," his mother said, "not from some teacher in a classroom. And," she continued, "it's no use dreaming about what you'll become. You just have to take what's given you and be satisfied."

Mrs. Pike stormed over to her son. "Aren't you satisfied with what I'm giving you? Haven't I worked hard?" She knocked his books off the chair without giving him a chance to answer. "Until you leave this house, you'd better shape up. Quit your fancy notions and get your chores done."

"Maybe I'll run away," Bill said under his breath. "Then I can find someone who will understand me."

"I'm your mother, remember? I understand you all too well. Get up to your room and stay there until you realize just how good you've got it. If you come down before 5:30, we'll eat together. Otherwise, make yourself a sandwich. I have to work tonight. One of the girls is sick, so I'm working part of her shift."

Bill walked up the creaky stairs and picked up the binoculars he'd won in the science fair. *If I just do the chores and watch television all evening without learning anything new, Mom will probably tell me my conduct is improving.* He threw an eraser against the wall. *Who says I can't grow up to be somebody?*

A gust of wind rattled the windowpane and flung snow against the glass. *How am I supposed to shovel the driveway when it's still snowing?* He jerked the $20 bill his grandfather had sent him for Christmas out of its hiding place behind the dresser and put on his winter clothes. *Mom needs to realize that I can make it on my own, without her help. Then she won't have to feed me until I get old enough to be kicked out.* Stifling his loneliness and frustration, Bill crept downstairs. *I'm sure glad she turned up the television.*

A savage wind blew sheets of snow into his face when he stepped outside. No matter how he tied his scarf, the wind soon blew snow down his neck. While crossing a vacant lot, he fell into a snow-covered hole, and snow went inside his boots. Several times he actually fell down because the snow was almost too deep to walk through.

His lips blue with cold, Bill determined to keep going. He wiggled his numb toes and clapped his hands. When he reached the outskirts of town, he followed the telephone poles so he wouldn't get lost.

Only one car passed him as he neared Keeneyville. The town's sign was almost hidden by snow. *I'm almost there,* he thought, trudging steadily until he reached the bus station. Then he pushed on the door. It was locked! He peered through the frosted window, but it was dark inside. Clapping his mittens together, he walked completely around the building. There was no way in.

The wind crept under his jacket, and his cheeks hurt. *I have to get out of the cold or I might get frostbite.* Shivering, he walked back down the street.

After battling the wind and snow for two blocks,

Bill entered a small cafe. The blinking red sign said, "Anderson's."

"Hello there, young fellow." The man put a chair on a table and swept the floor underneath it. "I'm closing up, but I'll pour you some hot chocolate or something. What's your name?"

"Thanks. I'm Bill." He tried to unzip his frozen zipper with numb fingers.

"How come you're out on a night like this?" Mr. Anderson's questioning eyes looked Bill up and down. "The roads are all closed because of the drifting snow. I heard on the radio that the police are telling everyone not to drive."

"I was hoping to catch the bus to York City to stay with my aunt," Bill said, warming his hands on the hot chocolate cup. "Do you know how much a ticket costs?"

"Not offhand," said Mr. Anderson, getting out a dustpan. "It's not too bad, but with gas prices what they are and all, it's not going to be cheap either. If you're thinking about leaving tonight," the man continued, "better forget it. They closed the bus station more than two hours ago."

Bill stared blankly out the window, wondering what he'd do next.

"I don't mean to pry, Bill," Mr. Anderson said, "but aren't you kinda young to be out by yourself? How'd you get here?"

"I walked from Murryville," Bill said, trying to sound calm.

"That's more than five miles away!" the man exclaimed, not trying to hide his surprise. "You live there?"

"I used to."

90

"You know, I've got a boy about your age. He sometimes gets into things he doesn't know how to handle too. I guess we all do."

"Nobody can help me with this problem," Bill said, staring at the saltshaker. "It's my mother. She won't change, and she'll keep making things hard for me."

"Sometimes parents will change, and sometimes they won't," Mr. Anderson said. "Usually, though, they try to do their best."

"My mother doesn't," Bill said angrily, his eyes flashing. "When Dad left, she changed. She works six days a week, and when she gets home all she does is watch television and order me to do my chores."

"Television does pass the time when a person is bored," Mr. Anderson said. "Some people spend nearly all their time watching it instead of talking with other people or being creative."

"I used to build models, but my mother complained about the mess. She can't wait to get me out of the house so that she won't have to work as hard. And when I talk about getting a good job someday, she just calls me a 'dreamer.' "

"It's probably hard for your mother to dream dreams when she is working that many hours," Mr. Anderson said. "Maybe she's just tired and doesn't mean what she says."

"Oh, yes, she does," Bill stated firmly. "She repeats herself often enough."

"Maybe so," the man said, sitting down in the booth across from Bill. "But many people will try to keep you from dreaming because they think you'll just get hurt when your dreams don't come true."

"But my dreams are going to come true. I'm going

91

to get a good job when I get older, and my science teacher says that I ask good questions."

"I'm sure of that." Mr. Anderson smiled. "But it won't be easy for you. You may have to keep your dreams inside and stop sharing them with people, even your mother. Parents don't always understand their children's dreams. They may think dreams are only daydreams. Sometimes it's because they don't take time to listen to their children. Other times it's because they have seen their own dreams crumble." He turned off all but one of the lights. "Let me tell you about my dad, who owned a farm. I worked hard for him as I grew up. He wanted to retire there, but when the high interest rates came he couldn't afford to farm any longer. He moved to an apartment and died six months later. Dad had a dream, but through no fault of his own it fell through."

"But how about you?" Bill asked. "You've got this place." He watched the snow swirl around the street light.

"This place isn't perfect," the man said, "but I'm good at running it, and I have fun. Somebody else might not want to run it at all, but that's the way it should be. I saved for a long time to buy this cafe. It was my dream, not somebody else's. I wouldn't expect you to want to run this place. Even my son won't. He's learning things in school I never even thought about when I was his age. At first that scared me, but when I realized I could help him by encouraging him, I didn't feel that way any more."

"My mother doesn't listen to my dreams—all she cares about is my chores. But I'd rather learn about science."

" 'If you don't feed the cows,' my grandfather used

to say, 'they won't give milk.' Maybe if you did your chores well, your mother would have more faith in you. She might even change her mind about what you are learning." Mr. Anderson looked at the clock on the wall. "I've got to get home while I still can. Do you have someplace to go?"

Bill shook his head. "No, but I'm not going home."

"How about coming home with me, on the condition that we call your mother?"

"I don't have anything to say to her," Bill said. "She probably hasn't even missed me."

"What if I talk to her for you?"

"Well, if you want to, you can."

A few minutes later, in Mr. Anderson's small car, they were plowing through the drifts on a narrow lane. "We love it out here," Mr. Anderson said.

"It's pretty," Bill agreed.

As they entered the house and hurriedly shut the kitchen door, a woman called out, "Some night, isn't it, Andy?" Then she saw Bill. "Who is this?"

"Martha, this is Bill. He'll probably be staying with us tonight, after we call his mother."

"Fine," Mrs. Anderson said. "I'll put another plate on."

Mr. Anderson telephoned Bill's mother and explained that her son was safe. A few minutes later, he sat down in the living room. "Your mother is really concerned about you, Bill. She wanted to know when you will be home. She seems to love you a great deal."

"She sure hides it then," Bill said, trying to sound tough.

"Running away is a serious thing," Mr. Anderson said, "and it really doesn't solve anything. In fact, it usually makes things worse. Now you still have your original problem, plus you have undermined your mother's trust in you."

"What if she blames me for everything?"

"You have to fulfill your part of the bargain," Mr. Anderson advised. "Until you do your chores and demonstrate that you are thankful for what she is doing for you, you shouldn't expect her attitude to change."

"You don't know what it's like."

"Self-pity won't get you anywhere," Mr. Anderson said. "If you don't hang in there and try to make things better, there's not much that anybody can do for you. A lot of ugly things happen to runaways besides just being cold and hungry." Bill nodded and moved closer to the heating vent.

"Hi," a tall boy said as he entered the room. "I'm Loren. Mom told me you were here. I was working in the basement. Bet you could use some dry socks."

"I'm Bill." He followed Loren upstairs, and his eyes widened in amazement as he stepped into Loren's room. The dresser was piled high with science books!

"Have you read all these?" Bill asked.

"Most of them. I checked them out of the library."

"How long have you been interested in science?"

"A long time," Loren answered. "Dad used to cut trees for the forestry department, and he taught me a lot. So I started a science club at school. For a while, I was the only member. I took field trips by myself. But now there are six of us in the club."

"We don't have a club like that at my school," Bill answered. "Nobody else wants one."

"Then start one yourself. You can do it. Talk to your science teacher."

What could my first field trip be? Bill wondered. *In the spring, I could hunt for wild flowers in the woods.* He grinned. *But first there is a lot of snow to shovel.*

> Children, obey your parents; this is the right thing to do because God has placed them in authority over you. . . . And now a word to you parents. Don't keep on scolding and nagging your children, making them angry and resentful. Rather, bring them up with the loving discipline the Lord himself approves, with suggestions and godly advice.
>
> Ephesians 6:1,4 LB

Lord, there are many kids who only have one parent, and I know that's not easy. Please help me understand my family better and be willing to pitch in when something needs to be done. Thank you that I can dream dreams. And help me remember that I can't solve my problems by running away from them. I have to work them out, and I need to ask you to help me do that.

I Want to Be Somebody

"OK, Tom, it's your turn. What type of job would you like to have when you're older?"

Tom gave his friends a knowing look. "Mr. Turnbull, I want to be a professional football player because they make lots of money and people look up to them." He flexed his muscles, and several girls giggled.

"How about you, Peter?"

Peter thought for a moment. "I want to work in physical therapy, helping people learn how to move their arms and legs."

A girl behind Peter whispered across the aisle, "That's what my sister wants to be."

"If they're not smart enough to know how to move their arms or legs," Tom said in a voice meant to be heard, "how can someone help them?"

"That's enough, Tom," Mr. Turnbull said. "Now, how about you, Ellen?"

After class, Tom and several of his friends hurried to the locker room. Minutes later, they began playing basketball in the gym. "We sure need to beat Ridgewood this weekend," Tom said. "We can't let them be conference champs two years in a row." He ran down the floor and made a lay-up.

"If you keep playing like you did last week, we'll do fine," Matthew, a tall boy, said. "You made the forward on the Central team look silly. You just ran circles around him."

"He did look foolish, didn't he?" Tom grinned. "But I've got to keep practicing. If I'm going to be anybody, I've got to keep working hard and prove how good I am."

"You work too hard," another boy said. "You never have time to go bike riding or anything."

Tom stopped shooting baskets. "I have other things to do." He paused. "You can't make good grades without studying a lot, and nobody gives you anything. If you don't just go out and get what you want, you'll end up with nothing."

"Maybe," the boy said, "but I don't want success if I have to work that hard for it."

"Me, I admit I want success," Tom said. "I want to do my best. I'm going to earn respect."

Matthew threw Tom a basketball. "You don't have to be so serious about it. Besides, who knows what success is, anyway? My dad's friend thought that success was making lots of money, and he died of a heart attack a month ago."

"Maybe he didn't get enough exercise," Tom snapped. "Hey, I let you guys think the way you want to. Let me think my way. In the meantime, I'll make sure that Ridgewood knows I'm in the game."

"I'm sure you will," the other boy said. "But don't forget it's still a game, OK? It's meant to be fun too."

After basketball practice, Matthew's mother picked Tom up too. As they were riding home, Matthew said, "Hey, look. There's Peter Hawkins, and he's jogging in that field."

Tom looked closely. "Look at how he runs. He looks weird."

"He hasn't been in gym class," Matthew said. "I heard that he was in an accident during summer vacation, but I haven't asked him about it."

"I didn't hear anything about it," Tom replied.

The next day, Tom walked up to Peter in the hallway. "Hey, I saw you running last night." Tom ran a short way down the hall, twisting his body and keeping a stiff leg. "Where'd you learn to run like that?"

Peter smiled. "That does look funny, doesn't it? I've never seen myself run, but I've wondered how I look. Do I really look like that?"

Tom gave Peter a surprised look. "Not quite that bad," he said. Then he walked away.

Later that evening, as Tom crossed the street near his house, he heard the screech of brakes. He glanced up. *What's that? I have the "walk" sign. They have to stop.* But the car didn't stop. It hit him a glancing blow and threw him into the air.

The next thing Tom knew, he was in a hospital bed. "Oh, you're awake," the nurse said. "Your parents just left. We thought you'd stay asleep."

Tom looked down at the cast on his leg. "What happened?"

"A guy ran the light," the nurse answered. "Your leg is broken in two places, but you're lucky to be alive."

"Can I have some water?" Tom shut his eyes. "I'm so sleepy."

"We're giving you medicine for pain. Go back to sleep."

At school the next day, the principal announced over the intercom that Tom had been hurt. "He'll be in the hospital for a while," the principal said, "and after tomorrow he can have visitors."

Two days later, as Tom sipped some water, someone knocked at the door. "Come in."

Peter stepped awkwardly inside the door. "I thought you might, uh, want some company, so I stopped by. The nurse said you were awake."

"Yeah. It seems like all I do is sleep," Tom complained. "And when I'm not sleeping, they're asking me lots of questions and giving me medicine."

"How's your leg?"

"How should I know?" Tom snapped. "I can't even see it very well. They put it in this cast." He lay his head back down on the pillow and sighed heavily. "I'm sorry, Peter. I'm just really tired of this room. I can't wait to get out of here."

"When will that be?" Peter asked.

"The doctor won't say," Tom said.

Peter looked thoughtfully out the window. "I know how you feel."

"Do you really?" Tom asked. "For no reason a car hits me and breaks my leg in two places, and I can't do anything but lie in this bed."

"I was in the hospital too," Peter said. "A bus skidded and hit our car when we were coming back from Philadelphia." His voice broke. "My sister was killed, and my hip was fractured." He pointed. "The big bone right here broke."

"I didn't know," Tom said. "I'm sorry."

"That's OK," Peter said quietly. "Most people don't. It happened during summer vacation."

"Are you all right now?" Tom asked.

"I'm getting better," Peter said. "The doctor just told me last week that I could run one block a night. He wants to see how I do. I run funny, but I'm glad I can run."

"My doctor says I'll have to wear this cast for weeks," Tom said. "Both bones were broken, and I might have to have a pin in my leg." He gripped the sides of the bed. "Me, with a pin in my leg, just like a cripple."

"Hey, watch what you say," Peter said, grinning. "I've got more than just a pin in my body. At first the doctors didn't think I would live, but I did. And I'm not exactly a cripple, even though I can't do everything other kids can do."

"But I want to make something of myself," Tom said. "I want to show people how good I am in what I do so they'll pay attention to me. I'm not going to fail."

"Failing in something isn't always bad," Peter said. "We can't do everything, you know."

"I can," Tom stated in a determined voice, "and I'm going to prove that to everybody."

"Maybe," Peter said, "but people are valuable because of who they are as persons, not for what they accomplish. If I am only valuable because of what I do, then I've got problems. I'm not the best student in the world, and because of my hip I'll never be great in sports. But maybe I can do something special for other people. Maybe what I've been through has taught me something that will help me make life easier for someone else."

"If you just came in here to preach at me, forget it." Tom's voice rose. "I'm going to miss the Ridgewood game and a lot of other things just because of one guy's bad driving. Why did it happen to me?"

"Things like this happen all the time," Peter said. He took several steps. "Hey, I didn't mean to bug you. I just thought you might want some company."

"My leg is killing me," Tom said. He turned his head toward the window.

Nearly a week later, Peter saw a crowd of kids standing in the doorway at school. "It's Tom," Matthew called out. "He's here." Peter watched with the others as Tom squeezed his crutches through the side door, but he stood at a distance. *I don't think he wants to see me. I might just make him mad again.*

Later that morning, Peter rounded a corner and nearly bumped into Tom. Several boys were standing beside Tom, giving him suggestions. "Why don't you move that leg up there?" one said.

"I tried that already," Tom said, "and if I don't get up these stairs soon I'm going to be late for class."

"Hey, I know how to get you up those stairs," Peter said.

"Yeah, I guess you would know that. Will you show me?"

"Sure." Peter showed Tom how to maneuver the crutches, and they walked into class together.

"What are you doing with Peter?" Matthew whispered as Tom sat down beside him.

"He helped me carry my books," Tom said. "What's it to you?"

"Tom, if I didn't know you so well, I'd think you liked Peter."

"I do. Ease up on him. He's an all right guy. I understand now why he's interested in physical therapy." Tom looked down at his cast. "Maybe being a pro football player wouldn't be that great after all."

> Be kind and compassionate to one another.
>
> Ephesians 4:32 NIV

It's not easy to love other people and be kind to them all the time, Lord. But you love me a lot, and you can give me the ability to love other people even when I don't want to. Thank you that I don't have to earn your love or prove anything to you. Help me accept myself the way you have created me, and teach me that a lot of things are more important than being famous or making lots of money.

I Don't Want to Move

John laid his spelling book on the desk and walked out into the hallway. A moment later, he entered the kitchen. *These cookies sure are good,* he thought, popping one into his mouth. He could hear voices coming from the study and walked closer to hear who was speaking.

"So you see, Nancy, things could get pretty rough. Because I didn't take the promotion, I could be in the middle, especially if they make changes in the department." John's father spoke firmly.

"What will we do?" his mother asked. "We just ordered the new carpeting."

Without waiting to hear more, John hurried back to his room. *They can't do that to Dad,* he thought angrily. *He has worked for them for a long time, and he works hard. He said one time that sales weren't as good as they could be, but that's no reason not to promote him.* He sat down on his bed. *What'll happen if*

Dad loses his job? We might have to move. He tried to learn his spelling words, but he couldn't get his parents' conversation out of his mind.

"It's time to eat, John." Carol stuck her head inside the door. "How's it going?"

He frowned. "I'm having a hard time."

"Maybe I can help you," his sister said. "I'm pretty good at spelling."

"It's not that I can't do it," John said. "It's just that. . . ."

"Just what?" his sister asked.

"Never mind," John said. "Let's eat." He and his sister walked downstairs and sat down at the kitchen table.

After the prayer, his mother began to pass the food. John took small helpings of everything, including his favorite meatloaf.

"How come you're so quiet tonight?" his father asked. "Have a hard day at school?"

"It was all right," John said. "I'm just not hungry."

Mrs. Flood gave him a strange look. "You're not getting that flu, are you? Seems like everybody in the neighborhood is getting it."

"No, Mom. I'm fine. I really am." To emphasize his point, John took a big mouthful of carrots.

"That's good," Mr. Flood said, "because I'm going to need your help with a special project this weekend. I'm finally going to clean out the garage, and I want you and Carol to help me. Because it'll take a few extra hours, I'll double your allowances this week."

"Now I'll be able to buy that record album," Carol said, "the one I told you about, Mom." She poured another glass of milk. "I hope it won't take all day, though. I told Barb that I'd come over about 2:00."

"I don't want extra money," John suddenly said, his eyes intense. "You don't have to pay me."

"I know I don't have to," his father said, "but I want to. With our vacation coming up, I thought you might need a little extra money."

"I don't need more money, and Carol doesn't either."

"What do you mean?" Carol gave him a dirty look. "Why'd you say that?"

"What's gotten into you tonight, John?" his mother said. "You're not your usual smiling self."

"I'm sorry." John put his napkin on the table. "Can I be excused?"

"Sure."

John went back to his room and started playing with his chemistry set. An hour later, there was a knock on his door.

"Mrs. Falter is on the phone," his mother said, "and she wants to know if you want to ride with them to the hayride on Saturday night."

"I've decided not to go," John replied. "It costs too much."

"We'll be glad to pay for it," Mrs. Flood said. "You know we're willing to help out with things like that. All you have to do is ask."

"I don't want to go," John repeated. "The hay makes me sneeze."

"All right, I'll tell Mrs. Falter. But if you change your mind, let her know."

John listened as his mother walked downstairs. *I like it here,* he thought. *I don't want to move. Why did this have to happen to Dad?* He thought about the boxes of canned food that the church was col-

107

lecting for members whose unemployment compensation was running out.

At school the next day, he sat down at the corner table in the cafeteria and several boys joined him.

"Did you see the new go-cart Doug got for his birthday?" Ralph asked. "He was driving it up and down the paths in Lawson Field all day yesterday. I wish I could have one. It's more fun than a bicycle."

"Dad told me last night that we're going to buy a swimming pool." Sammy grinned. "We'll all be able to use it. It'll have a heater so that the water will always be the right temperature."

John didn't say anything. He kept thinking about what it would be like to move away. *It doesn't seem fair,* he thought. *Why do some people keep making lots of money and others lose their jobs? Doesn't God pay attention to who is really working hard?* John thought about all the times his father had come home late for dinner. Then John wished that he could get a job and earn money to help his father.

At the dinner table, he brought up the subject of getting a job. "Dad, do you know somebody who would hire me to do odd jobs? I could mow the grass, pull weeds, and other things like that."

"I'm sure people need that kind of work done," his father replied. "But why are you thinking about working all of a sudden? When I talked to you last week about mowing the lawn, you acted like it was the worst job in the world."

"I've changed my mind," John said. "I want to earn some money."

"That reminds me, Mother," Carol interrupted. "I need money to buy some new clothes. All the other girls are wearing new spring outfits."

108

"You don't need clothes that badly," John stated. "You're always asking for money to buy clothes."

"That's not true," Carol answered. "I haven't bought any clothes for a while. Besides, who made you the expert on who needs clothes? I was talking to Mother."

"Carol is right, John," Mrs. Flood said. "It really isn't your business."

"I'm sorry," John said quickly. "It's just that clothes cost a lot of money."

"You let us worry about that," Mrs. Flood said.

"John," Mr. Flood said, "would you like a new bicycle for your birthday? Your old one is too small for you, and I've noticed that many of your friends have ten-speeds."

"Ten-speeds cost too much," John replied. "I really don't need a new bicycle."

"Is he sick or something?" Carol asked, looking at John. "Since when does he turn down a new bicycle?"

"You don't understand." John hurried to his room.

"Let him go," Mr. Flood said as his wife started to say something. "I'll talk with him later."

After dinner, Mr. Flood invited John to the study and closed the door. "John, for the past several days you've been acting different. First you decided not to go on the hayride. Then you talked about mowing lawns when you hate mowing lawns. Now you tell us that you don't want a new bicycle!"

John nodded. "I, uh, heard you and Mom talking about your job, and I thought you would need all the money. I don't want to move," he added. "I like it here."

"So that's it." His father smiled. "You heard me telling your mother about not accepting the promotion, and you thought we'd run out of money and have to move."

"That's happening to many people," John said earnestly. "In my English class, Mrs. Sherman talked about all the people who can't find jobs. Why didn't you take the new job? You work hard, and you've been working there a long time."

"I've done well in sales," Mr. Flood said slowly, "but not every person who can sell things can manage other salesmen. The truth is, I turned down the promotion because I knew I'd be happier where I am. I don't want to be cooped up in an office every day."

"But you'd have gotten more money, wouldn't you?"

"Yes, but money isn't everything. I love what I'm doing, and all the money in the world won't make me do something I can't enjoy or do well in. God has always taken care of us, and he won't stop now."

"But how will you pay for the carpeting?" John asked.

"We'll wait and buy it another time."

"You can use the money you were going to spend on my bicycle for the carpeting."

Mr. Flood put his arm around John. "No, I won't do that. You are special to us, and we want to buy you something special."

"But I don't need a new bicycle. I could get a used one instead."

"John, I tell you what. Let's go to the police auction and pick out several bicycles you might like. Then we can bid on them and see which one we get. We can use the money we save to buy food for the canned food drive at church. Even though I didn't take the promotion, we still have a lot to be thankful for."

"We sure do," John said. "Let's go get some cookies. I'm starved."

> Do not be anxious about anything, but in everything, by prayer and petition, with thanksgiving, present your requests to God. And the peace of God, which transcends all understanding, will guard your hearts and your minds in Christ Jesus.
>
> Philippians 4:6-7 NIV

It's hard for me to understand how much you care about me and my family, Lord, but you do. Thank you for listening to my prayers and for promising to give me your peace whenever I start worrying about anything. Please teach me how to trust you more.